Woodland Christmas

Woodland Christmas

Twelve Days of Christmas in the North Woods

by

FRANCES TYRRELL

Scholastic Press

New York

**The illustrations for this book were done
in watercolor on Arches rag paper.**

Copyright © 1995 by Frances Tyrrell

All rights reserved. Published by Scholastic Press,
a division of Scholastic Inc., *Publishers since 1920,*
555 Broadway, New York, NY 10012, by arrangement with
Scholastic, Ltd.

Library of Congress Cataloging-in-Publication Data

Woodland Christmas (English folk song)
Woodland Christmas / by Frances Tyrrell.
p.   cm.
Summary: Illustrations depicting the courtship of two black bears
in a woodland setting accompany the words to the traditional
Christmas song.
ISBN 0-590-86367-3
1. Folk songs, English — England — Texts. 2. Christmas music —
Texts. [1. Folk songs — England. 2. Christmas music.]
I. Tyrrell, Frances.
PZ8.3.T8517   1996
782.42 — dc20
[E]   95-44506
CIP
AC

12 11 10 9 8 7 6 5 4 3 2 1   6 7 8 9/9 0 1/0
Printed in the U.S.A.   37
First United States printing, October 1996

Typeset in Galliard

For our little cub, Neil.

The animals in this book are:
one gray partridge,
two rock doves, three ruffed grouse,
four common loons, five river otters,
six Canada geese, seven whistling swans, eight raccoons,
nine red foxes, ten moose, eleven red squirrels,
and twelve beavers.
The bird in the potted pear tree
is a California partridge,
and the courting couple are black bears.

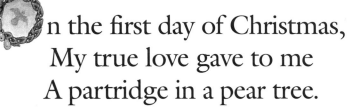

On the first day of Christmas,
My true love gave to me
A partridge in a pear tree.

On the second day of Christmas,
My true love gave to me:
Two turtledoves
And a partridge in a pear tree.

On the third day of Christmas,
My true love gave to me:
Three French hens
Two turtledoves
And a partridge in a pear tree.

On the fourth day of Christmas,
My true love gave to me:
Four calling birds
Three French hens
Two turtledoves
And a partridge in a pear tree.

5   5

On the fifth day of Christmas,
My true love gave to me:
Five golden rings
Four calling birds
Three French hens
Two turtledoves
And a partridge in a pear tree.

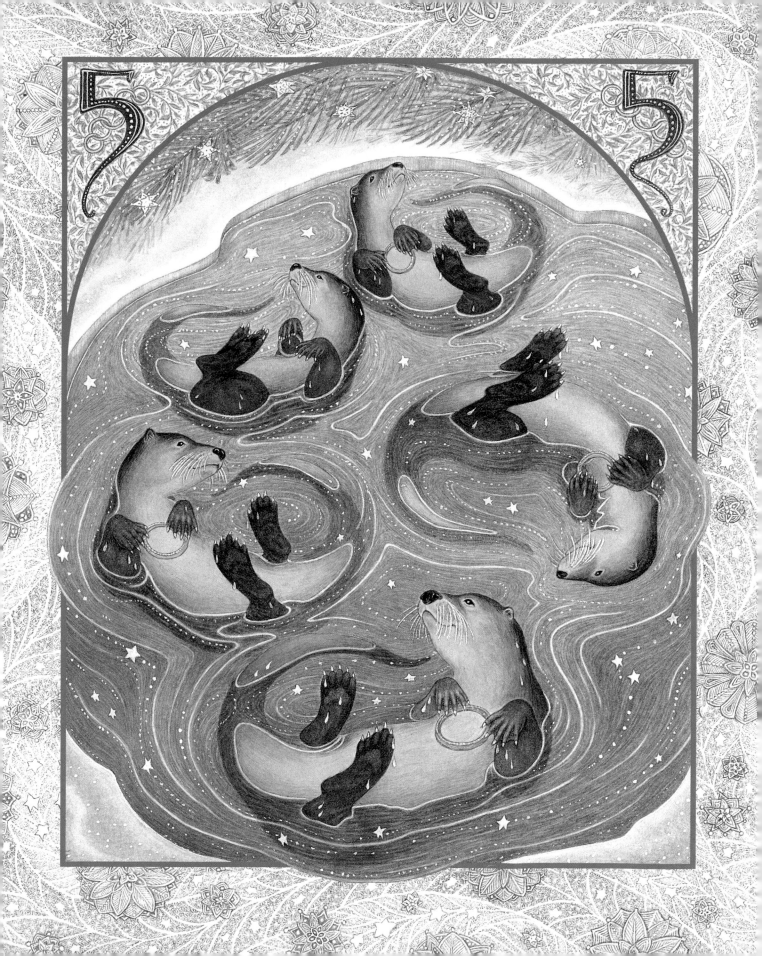

On the sixth day of Christmas,
My true love gave to me:
Six geese a-laying
Five golden rings
Four calling birds
Three French hens
Two turtledoves
And a partridge in a pear tree.

On the seventh day of Christmas,
My true love gave to me:
Seven swans a-swimming
Six geese a-laying
Five golden rings
Four calling birds
Three French hens
Two turtledoves
And a partridge in a pear tree.

On the eighth day of Christmas,
My true love gave to me:
Eight maids a-milking
Seven swans a-swimming
Six geese a-laying
Five golden rings
Four calling birds
Three French hens
Two turtledoves
And a partridge in a pear tree.

On the ninth day of Christmas,
My true love gave to me:
Nine ladies dancing
Eight maids a-milking
Seven swans a-swimming
Six geese a-laying
Five golden rings
Four calling birds
Three French hens
Two turtledoves
And a partridge in a pear tree.

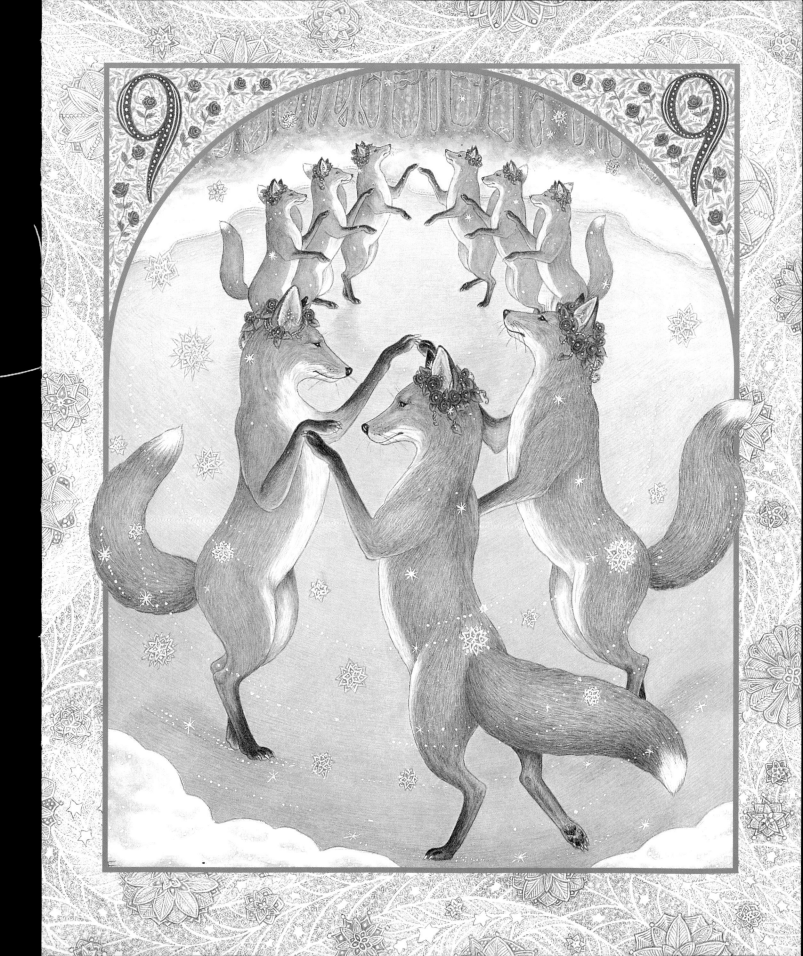

On the tenth day of Christmas,
My true love gave to me:
Ten lords a-leaping
Nine ladies dancing
Eight maids a-milking
Seven swans a-swimming
Six geese a-laying
Five golden rings
Four calling birds
Three French hens
Two turtledoves
And a partridge in a pear tree.

On the eleventh day of Christmas,
My true love gave to me:
Eleven pipers piping
Ten lords a-leaping
Nine ladies dancing
Eight maids a-milking
Seven swans a-swimming
Six geese a-laying
Five golden rings
Four calling birds
Three French hens
Two turtledoves
And a partridge in a pear tree.

On the twelfth day of Christmas,
My true love gave to me:
Twelve drummers drumming
Eleven pipers piping
Ten lords a-leaping
Nine ladies dancing
Eight maids a-milking
Seven swans a-swimming
Six geese a-laying
Five golden rings
Four calling birds
Three French hens
Two turtledoves
And a partridge in a pear tree.

7410